Cupcakes

igloobooks

Published in 2013
by Igloo Books Ltd
Cottage Farm
Sywell
NN6 0BJ
www.igloobooks.com

Food photography and recipe development: PhotoCuisine UK
Front and back cover images © PhotoCuisine UK

HUN001 0413
4 6 8 10 9 7 5 3
ISBN 978-0-85780-729-8

Printed and manufactured in China

Cupcakes

Contents

Decadent

Cupcakes with Pistachios

MAKES
24

PREP TIME
20-30 minutes

COOKING TIME
20 minutes

INGREDIENTS

For the cupcakes

200 g / 7 oz / 1 cup butter, softened
200 g / 7 oz / 1 cup caster sugar
250 g / 9 oz / 1 ¼ cups self-raising flour
4 medium eggs
3 tbsp chopped pistachios
24 cupcake cases

To decorate

200 g / 7 oz / 1 cup white chocolate, chopped
100 g / 2 ½ oz / ½ cup chopped pistachios

METHOD

Preheat oven to 180°C (160° fan) 375F, gas 5.

Line 2 cupcake tins with paper cases.

Beat the butter and sugar together with an electric whisk until pale and fluffy.

Gradually add the eggs a little at a time beating thoroughly after each addition.

Spoon mixture into cases until nearly full.

Bake in the oven for 18-20 minutes until firm to the touch.

Cool on a wire rack.

To decorate, gently heat the chocolate in a heatproof bowl over a pan of simmering water.

With a spoon gently drizzle the chocolate over the cupcakes and garnish with the chopped pistachios.

Almond Chocolate Cupcakes

MAKES
12

PREP TIME
20 minutes

COOKING TIME
20 minutes

INGREDIENTS

For the cupcakes

100 g / 3 ½ oz / ¾ cup self-raising flour, sifted
150 g / 5 oz / ¾ cup golden caster (superfine)sugar
40 g / 1 ½ oz / ¼ cup softened butter
30 g / 1 oz cocoa powder
120 ml / 1 fl. oz whole milk
1 large egg
½ tsp vanilla essence
12 cupcake cases

To decorate

70 ml / 2 ½ fl. oz / ⅓ cup whole milk
225 g / 8 oz dark chocolate chopped
30 ml / 1 fl. oz double cream
55 g / 2oz butter
15 g / ½ oz powdered glucose
4 tbsp sugar syrup
100g / 3 ½ oz / 1 cup flaked almonds (slivered almonds)

METHOD

Preheat the oven to 180°C (160° fan) 375F, gas 5.

Line a cupcake tin with 12 paper cases.

Sift the flour and baking powder into a food processor, add the butter and blend together until sandy in texture.

Add the eggs, sugar, vanilla and cocoa powder to the mix and blend again until incorporated.

Fill the paper cases with the mixture and bake for 15-20 minutes until cooked and well risen. Leave to cool on a wire rack.

To make the chocolate ganache, heat the milk until boiling and add the chocolate, cream, butter and glucose. Reduce the heat to low and stir until the chocolate has melted and it is well mixed. Add the sugar syrup.

Allow the icing to cool to a coating consistency.

Use a palette knife to top each of the cooled cupcakes with the ganache.

Decorate with the flaked almonds.

Hot Chocolate Cupcakes

MAKES
12

PREP TIME
45
minutes

COOKING TIME
15-20
minutes

INGREDIENTS

For the cupcakes

110 g / 4 oz / 1 cup self-raising flour, sifted

28 g / 1 oz / ¼ cup unsweetened cocoa powder, sifted

110 g / 4 oz / ½ cup caster (superfine) sugar

110 g / 4 oz / ½ cup butter, softened

2 large eggs

225 g / 8 oz dark chocolate, minimum 60% cocoa solids

For the garnish

225 ml / 8 fl. oz / 1 cup double (heavy) cream

2 tbsp icing (confectioners') sugar

mixed summer berries

METHOD

Preheat the oven to 190°C (170° fan) / 375F / gas 5 and oil 12 small mugs.

Combine the flour, cocoa, sugar, butter and eggs in a bowl and whisk together for 2 minutes or until smooth.

Divide half the mixture between the mugs.

Break the chocolate into squares and divide between the mugs, then spoon the rest of the cake mixture on top.

Sit the mugs on a baking tray and bake in the oven for 15 – 20 minutes.

Test with a wooden toothpick, if it comes out clean, the cakes are done.

While the cakes are cooking, make the topping. Whisk the cream with the icing sugar until thick and spoon into a piping bag fitted with a large star nozzle.

When the cakes are ready, pipe a swirl of cream on top and scatter over a few summer berries.

Double Chocolate Cupcakes

MAKES
15

PREP TIME
30
minutes

COOKING TIME
20
minutes

INGREDIENTS

For the cupcakes

90 g / 3 oz / ¾ cup unsalted butter, softened
50 g / 1 ¾ oz / ½ cup dark chocolate,
finely chopped
100 g / 3 ½ oz / ¾ cup plain
(all-purpose) flour
½ tsp baking powder
½ tsp bicarbonate of (baking) soda
50 g / 1 ¾ oz / ½ cup ground almonds
140 g / 5 oz / ¾ cup dark muscovado sugar
½ tsp vanilla extract
2 medium eggs, lightly beaten
75 ml / 3 fl. oz / ½ cup buttermilk

To decorate

200 g / 1 cup unsalted butter, softened
50 g / 1 ¾ oz / ½ cup cocoa powder
200 g / 7oz / 1 cup icing sugar, sifted
tub of sprinkles

METHOD

Preheat the oven to 180°C (160° fan) 375F, gas 5.

Line the cupcake trays with 15 paper cases.

Place the chocolate in a bowl and pour over 60 ml of just boiled water. Stir until melted, then set aside to cool.

In a bowl, sift together the flour, baking powder and bicarbonate, then stir in the ground almonds.

In another bowl use an electric mixer to cream together the butter and sugar until very light and fluffy.

Add the eggs and vanilla extract slowly to the creamed butter and sugar mix.

Add a little flour to the mixture to prevent curdling.

Add the melted chocolate and the buttermilk then fold in the remaining flour and spoon the mixture into the paper cases.

Cook for 18-20 minutes until firm to the touch.

Remove from the tin and allow to cool on a wire rack.

To make the buttercream, cream together the butter and icing sugar until light and fluffy and then add the cocoa powder.

Using a palette knife, scoop the buttercream onto the cupcakes and scatter over the sprinkles to garnish.

Chocolate Ball Cupcakes

MAKES
12

PREP TIME 20 minutes

COOKING TIME 18-20 minutes

INGREDIENTS

For the cupcakes

100 g / 3 ½ oz / ⅔ cup self-raising flour, sifted
150 g / 5 oz / ¾ cup golden caster (superfine) sugar
40 g / 1 ½ oz / ¼ cup softened butter
20 g / ¾ oz cocoa powder
120 ml / 1 fl. oz / ¼ cup whole milk
1 tbsp malted milk
1 large egg
½ tsp vanilla essence
12 cupcake cases

To decorate

12 chocolate honeycomb balls
225 g / 8 oz / 1 ½ cups icing sugar, sifted

METHOD

Preheat the oven to 180°C (160° fan) 375F, gas 5. Line a cupcake tin with 12 cases.

Using a food processor, blend the sugar and butter together until pale and creamy. Add the cocoa powder and the malted milk. Pour in half of the milk and blend.

In a separate bowl, mix together the egg and vanilla essence. Add the mixture from the food processor and mix together.

Spoon the mixture into the cupcake cases and bake for 18 - 20 minutes until firm to the touch. Leave to cool on a wire rack.

Mix the icing sugar with a little water to produce a thick pouring consistency and spoon onto the cupcakes. Decorate with a chocolate honeycomb ball.

Maraschino Cherry Cupcakes

MAKES
24

PREP TIME
15
minutes

COOKING TIME
15
minutes

INGREDIENTS

For the cupcake
225 g / 8 oz / 1 ½ cups self-raising flour
175 g / 6 oz / 1 cup caster (superfine) sugar
3 tsp baking powder
Pinch of salt
175 g / 6 oz / ¾ cup unsalted butter, softened
90 g / 3 oz cherry puree
4 medium egg whites
30 ml / 1 fl. oz milk

To decorate
2 jars of maraschino cherries

METHOD

Preheat the oven to 180°C (160° fan) 375F, gas 5.

Line a cupcake tray with paper cases.

With a wooden spoon stir together the sifted flour, sugar, baking powder and salt.

With an electric beater add the cherry puree and softened butter until the batter is thick and creamy.

In another bowl whisk the egg whites together with the milk until lightly frothy.

Fold the egg mixture gently into the batter mix until fully incorporated.

Spoon into the paper cases.

Bake for 15 minutes or until well risen and dark golden.

Leave to cool on a wire rack.

Decorate each cupcake with a maraschino cherry.

Pistachio and Coffee Cupcakes

MAKES
24

PREP TIME
20-30 minutes

COOKING TIME
20 minutes

INGREDIENTS

For the cupcakes

200 g / 7 oz / 1 cup butter, softened
200 g / 7 oz / 1 cup caster (superfine) sugar
250 g / 9 oz / 1 ¼ cups self-raising flour
4 medium eggs
3 tbsp strong coffee
24 green cupcake cases

To decorate

150 g / 5 oz / ¾ cup softened butter
300 g / 10 oz / 2 cups icing sugar, sifted
75 ml / 2 ½ fl. oz very strong coffee
2 tbsp cocoa powder
100 g / 3 ½ oz / 1 cup pistachios, shelled and chopped
100 g / 3 ½ oz / 1 cup chocolate covered coffee beans

METHOD

Preheat oven to 180°C (160° fan) 375F, gas 5.

Line 2 cupcake tins with green cases.

Beat the butter and sugar together with an electric whisk until pale and fluffy.

Gradually add the eggs a little at a time beating thoroughly after each addition.

Add the coffee then fold in the flour.

Spoon the mixture into the cases until nearly full.

Bake in the oven for 18-20 minutes until firm to the touch.

Cool on a wire rack.

Make the topping by beating the butter and sugar until light and airy.

Add the coffee and the cocoa powder to the buttercream.

Using a piping bag and star shaped nozzle pipe the buttercream in a circular motion onto the cupcakes.

Decorate with the pistachios and chocolate covered coffee beans.

Raspberry and Coconut Cupcakes

MAKES
6

PREP
TIME
30
minutes

COOKING
TIME
30
minutes

INGREDIENTS

For the cupcakes

200 g / 7 oz / 1 ½ cups self-raising flour
1 tsp baking powder
100 g / 3 ½ oz / ½ cup caster (superfine) sugar
200 ml / 7 fl. oz / 1 cup coconut milk
40 g / 1 ½ oz / ½ cup dessicated coconut
1 large egg, beaten
100 g / 3 ½ oz unsalted butter, melted
100 g / 3 ½ oz raspberries

To decorate

2 large egg whites
50 ml / 2 fl. oz water
100 g / 3 ½ oz / ½ cup caster sugar
icing sugar, for dusting
150 ml / 6 fl. oz / ½ cup double cream,
lightly whipped
6 tbsp raspberry jam

METHOD

Preheat the oven to 180°C (160° fan) 375F, gas 5.

Line a cupcake tin with paper cases and grease the other 6 holes in the tray.

Place all of the ingredients, except the raspberries, into a bowl and mix well.

Spoon the mixture into the cupcake cases and the greased cupcake moulds.

Place 2 raspberries into each of the cupcake cases. Leave the other 6 cupcakes plain.

Bake in the oven for 25 minutes until golden and risen.

Leave to cool on a wire rack. Remove the cupcakes without cases carefully to maintain their shape.

To make the meringue topping, beat the egg whites until stiff peaks appear.

Dissolve the sugar in the water and bring to the boil. Using an electric beater add the sugar syrup to the egg whites and beat continuously.

Pipe the meringue mixture onto the plain cupcakes and place under the grill to achieve a golden finish.

Spoon a little double cream and raspberry jam onto the raspberry cupcake and balance the meringue cupcake on top.

Chocolate and Chilli Cupcakes

INGREDIENTS

For the cupcakes

150 g / 5 ½ oz / 1 cup self-raising flour
2 ½ tsp cocoa powder
¾ tsp chilli powder
1 tsp baking powder
a pinch of salt
150 g / 5 ½ oz / ¾ cup unsalted butter, softened
265 g / 9 ½ oz / 1 ⅛ cups caster (superfine) sugar
120 g / 4 ½ oz / ½ cup dark chocolate, chopped
1 medium egg
12 paper cases or 12 silicone moulds

To decorate

chocolate sprinkles
mini chocolate balls
300 g / 11 oz / 6 cups icing (confectioner's) sugar, sifted
2 tbsp cocoa powder

METHOD

Preheat oven to 180°C (160° fan) 375F, gas 5.

Line cupcake tray with paper cases or use individual silicone moulds.

Sift the flour, cocoa powder, chilli pepper and salt into a mixing bowl.

Gently melt the butter together with the sugar and chocolate. Add 150 ml / 5 fl. oz water and whisk with a balloon whisk until combined. Leave to cool for a few minutes.

Add the egg to the cooled mixture then whisk in the dry ingredients.

Pour the mixture into the cases/moulds and bake for 25-30 minutes until well risen.

Leave to cool on a wire rack.

Make the topping by combining the icing sugar and cocoa powder and add enough water to produce a piping consistency.

Pipe the icing in a random fashion onto the cupcake.

Add sprinkles and chocolate balls for extra decoration.

Black Forest Cupcakes

MAKES
12

PREP TIME
30
minutes

COOKING TIME
20
minutes

INGREDIENTS

For the cupcakes

125 g / 4 ½ oz / ½ cup unsalted butter, softened
100 g / 3 ½ oz / ½ cup dark chocolate, chopped
300 g / 10 ½ oz / 1 cup cherry jam
2 large eggs, gently beaten
150 g / 5 oz / ⅔ cup caster (superfine) sugar
150 g / 5 oz / 1 cup self-raising flour
12 cupcake paper cases

To decorate

36 fresh cherries (12 whole, 24 chopped)
200 ml / 7 fl. oz double cream lightly whipped
1 tbsp icing sugar

METHOD

Preheat the oven to 180°C (160° fan) 375F, gas 5.

On a medium heat, melt the butter and then add the chocolate. Remove from the heat and stir until both are smooth and blended.

Add the jam, sugar, eggs and salt and stir together.

Fold in the flour and divide the mixture between the 12 paper cases.

Cook for 20-25 minutes until dark, golden and risen.

Leave to cool on a wire rack and remove from the tin.

Lightly whip the double cream with the icing sugar until it reaches piping consistency.

Stir through the chopped cherries and spoon in the mixture into the piping bag.

When the cakes have cooled, slice the tops off.

Pipe the cherry cream on top of the sliced cupcake and then place the top of the cake onto the cream.

Pipe more cream on top and decorate with a fresh cherry.

Apricot and Almond Cupcakes

MAKES 12

PREP TIME 20 minutes

COOKING TIME 20 minutes

INGREDIENTS

For the cupcakes

200 g / 7 oz / 1 ½ cups plain (all-purpose) flour

2 ½ tsp baking powder

110 g / 4 oz / ½ cup caster (superfine) sugar

½ tsp salt

125 g / 4 ½ oz / ½ cup chopped, dried apricots

90 ml / 1 ½ fl. oz / ¼ cup whole milk

90 ml / 1 ½ fl. oz / ¼ cup cottage cheese

80 ml / 3 fl. oz / ⅓ cup sunflower oil

1 medium egg

12 paper cases

To decorate

5 tbsp apricot jam (jelly)

225 g / 8 oz / 2 cups icing sugar, sifted

12 flaked (slivered) almonds

4 fresh apricots, cut into slivers

METHOD

Preheat oven to 200°C (170° fan) 400F, gas 6.

Place 12 paper cases in a 12-hole cup-cake tin.

Mix the flour, baking powder, salt and sugar together in a mixing bowl.

In a small bowl mix the milk, cottage cheese, oil and egg together.

Stir the wet ingredients into the dry together with the apricots. Stir until just combined.

Spoon the mixture into the cases and bake for 20 minutes until golden and risen.

Leave in the tins until cold, and then place on a wire rack.

To decorate, mix the apricot jam with a little icing sugar and a little water. Keep adding water until dropping consistency is reached.

Drizzle a little on each muffin and decorate with the flaked (slivered) almonds and a little sliver of fresh apricot (optional).

Campari Cupcakes

MAKES
12

PREP TIME
30 minutes

COOKING TIME
20-25 minutes

INGREDIENTS

For the cupcakes
175 g / 6 oz / ¾ cup unsalted butter, softened
175 g / 6 oz / ¾ cup golden caster
(superfine) sugar
3 large eggs
75 g / 3 oz grapefruit segments chopped
175 g / 6 oz / 1 cup self-raising flour

To decorate
115 g / 4 oz / ½ cup unsalted butter, softened
225 g / 8 oz / 1 ¾ cup icing sugar, sifted
2 tbsp Campari
pink food colouring

METHOD

Preheat the oven to 170°C (150° fan) 350F, gas 4.

Place the paper cases into the cupcake tray.

Beat the butter and sugar together in a bowl until creamy.

Gradually mix in the eggs, beating well after each addition.

Coat the grapefruit in a little of the flour and stir into the creamed mixture.

Fold in the remaining flour.

Pour the mixture into the paper cases and bake for 20-25 minutes.

Leave to cool on a wire rack.

To decorate beat the butter and sugar until light and fluffy. Stir in the Campari and beat again, add a little pink food colouring as desired.

Pipe the icing onto the cupcakes in a swirling motion. Scatter over the multicoloured sprinkles.

Valentine's Day Cupcakes

MAKES **10**

PREP TIME **30** minutes

COOKING TIME **25** minutes

INGREDIENTS

For the cupcakes

110 g / 4 oz / ½ cup unsalted butter, softened
85 g / 3 oz / ⅓ cup caster (superfine) sugar
2 tbsp light brown sugar
2 medium eggs
150 g / 5 oz / 1 cup plain (all-purpose) flour
25 g / 1 oz cocoa powder
1 tsp baking powder
a pinch of salt
120 ml / 4 fl. oz / ½ cup whole milk
85 g / 3 oz / ½ cup dark chocolate chips
10 paper cases

To decorate

150 g / 5 oz / ½ cup dark chocolate
3 tbsp whole milk
85 g / 3 oz / ⅓ cup unsalted butter
125 g / 4 ½ oz / 1 cup icing sugar
2 tbsp cocoa powder
sugar hearts for decoration

METHOD

Preheat oven to 190°C (170° fan) 375F, gas 5.

Place 10 paper cases into a cupcake tin.

Beat the butter and sugars together in a mixing bowl until light and fluffy.

Add the eggs a little at a time beating carefully.

Stir the dry ingredients until combined and gently stir into the butter mixture. Stir in the milk and chocolate chips.

Spoon the mixture into the paper cases and bake for around 25 minutes until risen and firm. Leave to cool before transferring to a wire rack.

To decorate, put the chocolate, milk and butter in a glass heat-resistant bowl set over a pan of simmering water and stir until melted. Leave to cool a little.

Sift the icing sugar into the chocolate mixture and beat until smooth.

Using a piping bag, pipe the icing in swirls over the cooled cupcakes and sprinkle with mini sugar hearts.

Rosewater Cupcakes

MAKES
12

PREP TIME
30 minutes

COOKING TIME
15-20 minutes

INGREDIENTS

For the cupcakes

110 g / 4 oz / ½ cup unsalted butter, softened
110 g / 4 oz / ½ cup caster (superfine) sugar
2 medium eggs, lightly beaten
110 g / 4 oz / ¾ cup self-raising flour
a pinch of salt
12 paper cases

To decorate

110 g / 4 oz / ½ cup unsalted butter, softened
225 g / 8 oz / 2 cups icing sugar, sifted
a few drops of pink food colouring
1 tsp rosewater
sugar flowers

METHOD

Preheat oven to 180°C (160° fan) 375F, gas 5.

Place paper cases into the cupcake tray.

Beat the sugar and butter until pale and creamy.

Add the eggs gradually and fold in the flour and salt until blended.

Spoon the mixture into the cases and bake for 15 - 20 minutes until golden and springy to the touch.

Leave to cool on a wire rack.

Beat the butter first before adding the icing sugar.

Add the rosewater and pink food colouring to the buttercream.

Pipe the buttercream in swirls onto the cupcakes and decorate with the sugar flowers.

Chocolate Cupcakes

MAKES **10**

PREP TIME **30** minutes

COOKING TIME **25** minutes

INGREDIENTS

For the cupcakes

110 g / 4 oz / ½ cup unsalted butter, softened
85 g / 3 oz / ½ cup caster (superfine) sugar
2 tbsp light brown sugar
2 medium eggs
150 g / 5 oz / 1 cup plain (all-purpose) flour
25 g / 1 oz cocoa powder
1 tsp baking powder
a pinch of salt
120 ml / 4 fl. oz / ½ cup whole milk
85 g / 3 oz / ½ cup dark chocolate, chopped
10 paper cases

To decorate

150 g / 5 oz / ¾ cup softened butter
300 g / 10 oz / 2 cups icing sugar, sifted
2 tbsp cocoa powder
chocolate cake sprinkles

METHOD

Pre-heat the oven to 190°C (170° fan) 375F, gas 5. Put 10 paper cases into a cupcake tin. Beat the butter and sugars together in a mixing bowl until light and fluffy.

Add the eggs a little at a time, beating carefully.

Stir in the dry ingredients until combined and gently stir in the butter mixture. Stir in the milk and chopped chocolate.

Spoon the mixture into the paper cases and bake for 25 minutes or until risen and firm. Leave to cool before transferring to a wire rack.

Make the topping by beating the butter, sugar and cocoa powder until light and airy.

Use a piping bag and star-shaped nozzle to pipe the buttercream in a circular motion onto the cupcakes.

Scatter over the chocolate cake sprinkles.

Pistachio and Cherry Cupcakes

MAKES
24

PREP TIME
20-30 minutes

COOKING TIME
20 minutes

INGREDIENTS

For the cupcakes

200 g / 7 oz / 1 cup butter, softened
200 g / 7 oz / 1 cup caster (superfine) sugar
250 g / 9 oz / 1 ¼ cups self-raising flour
4 medium eggs
3 tbsp chopped pistachios
24 cherries, pitted

To decorate

24 maraschino cherries
6 tbsp chopped pistachios
400 g / 7 oz / 1 cup unsalted butter
800 g / 14 oz / 3 cups icing sugar, sifted
1 tsp vanilla extract
white chocolate curls

METHOD

Preheat oven to 180°C (160° fan) 375F, gas 5.

Line 2 cupcake tins with paper cases.

Beat the butter and sugar together with an electric whisk until pale and fluffy.

Gradually add the eggs a little at a time beating thoroughly after each addition.

Add the chopped pistachios and spoon the mixture into the cases until half full.

Add a cherry to each cupcake then fill with the remaining mixture.

Bake in the oven for 18-20 minutes until firm to the touch.

Cool on a wire rack.

To decorate make the buttercream by beating the butter and sugar together until light and fluffy then add a little vanilla extract.

Pipe the buttercream onto the cupcakes and decorate each one with chopped pistachios, white chocolate curls and a maraschino cherry.

Coffee Religieuse Cake

MAKES
12

PREP
TIME
35
minutes

COOKING
TIME
20-30
minutes

INGREDIENTS

For the cupcakes

85 g / 3 oz / ⅓ cup butter
220 ml / 7 ½ fl. oz / 1 cup water
105 g / 3 ¾ oz / ⅔ cup plain four, well sifted
a pinch of salt
3 eggs, beaten
non-stick baking tray

To decorate

570 ml / 1 pint / 2 ½ cups double cream
2 tbsp icing (confectioner's) sugar
3 tbsp coffee essence
225 g / 8 oz / 1 cup icing sugar, sifted
2 tbsp very strong black coffee

METHOD

Preheat the oven to 200°C (fan 180°C) 400F, gas 6.

Put the butter and water into a heavy saucepan, heat slowly to melt the butter then turn up the heat and bring to a rolling boil.

Sieve the salt and flour 3 times.

When the mixture begins to boil, tip all the flour and salt into the pan and remove from the heat.

Working quickly, beat the mixture hard with a wooden spoon until the mixture leaves the side of the pan.

Spread the mixture onto a plate and leave to cool.

When the mixture is cooler return to the pan and beat in the eggs until soft, shiny and smooth.

The mixture should be dropping consistency and not runny.

Spoon onto a non-stick baking tray into 12 balls, with smaller balls of pastry placed on top of each ball.

Bake in the oven for 20-30 minutes until brown and firm.

Whip the cream, sugar and coffee essence together until thick and fill a piping bag.

To decorate, cut the top off each bun and pipe the coffee cream into the centres.

Mix the icing sugar with the hot coffee and beat with a wooden spoon until smooth and just runny.

Drizzle the coffee icing on top of each bun and pipe a little more of the coffee cream mixture around the edge and top for decoration.

Chocolate Blueberry Cupcakes

MAKES
14

PREP TIME
25 minutes

COOKING TIME
15 minutes

INGREDIENTS

For the cupcakes

150 g / 5 oz / ⅔ cup unsalted butter, softened
300 g / 11 oz / 1 ½ cups caster (superfine) sugar
3 eggs, lightly beaten
250 ml / 9 fl. oz / 1 ¼ cups whole milk
225 g / 8 oz plain (all-purpose) flour
a pinch of salt
1 tsp bicarbonate (baking) of soda
50 g / 1 ½ oz / ⅓ cup cocoa powder
50 g / 1 ½ oz / ⅓ cup fresh blueberries
14 cupcake cases

To decorate

110 g / 4 oz / ½ cup plain chocolate, chopped
150 g / 5 oz / ½ cup unsalted butter, softened
160 g / 6 oz / 1 ¼ cup icing (confectioner's) sugar, sifted
1 tsp vanilla extract
28 blueberries
a little icing sugar for sprinkling

METHOD

Preheat oven to 180°C (170° fan) 350F, gas 4.

Place 14 paper cases into a cupcake tin.

Beat the butter and sugar together in a mixing bowl until soft and creamy.

Add the eggs and milk a little at a time, beating carefully.

Sift in the flour, salt, bicarbonate of soda and cocoa, stir well to mix.

Spoon the mixture into the paper cases and bake for 15 minutes until firm.

Leave to cool.

To decorate, melt the chocolate in a bowl set over a pan of simmering water.

Once melted, leave to cool to room temperature.

Beat the butter in a bowl with an electric whisk until smooth and creamy.

Add the icing sugar and beat until light and fluffy.

Add the vanilla extract and melted chocolate and beat until smooth and velvety.

Spread the topping onto the cakes and decorate with blueberries and a little icing sugar to dust.

Giant Cupcake with Buttercream

MAKES
1

PREP TIME
40 minutes

COOKING TIME
1 hour 15 minutes

INGREDIENTS

For the cupcakes

175 g / 6 oz / ⅔ cup unsalted butter
175 g / 6 oz / 1 cup light muscovado sugar
3 large eggs, beaten
115 g / 4 oz / ¾ cup wholemeal self-raising flour
50 g / 2 oz / ⅓ cup plain (all-purpose) flour
2 tbsp cocoa powder
75 ml / 3 fl. oz / ⅓ cup whole milk

To decorate

120 g / 4 oz / ½ cup unsalted butter, softened
220 g / 8 oz / 1 ¼ cups icing sugar
200 g / 7 oz / 1 ½ cups fresh raspberries

METHOD

Preheat oven to 170°C (150° fan) 350F, gas 4.

Brush a giant cupcake mould with oil and dust with flour. Beat the butter and light muscovado sugar together in a bowl until creamy.

Gradually add the eggs, beating well after each addition.

Sieve together the wholemeal flour, plain flour and cocoa powder then stir into the mixture until evenly combined.

Finally stir in the milk.

Spoon the mixture into the mould and hollow out the centre a little.

Bake for 1 hour 15 minutes until a skewer pushed into the cake comes out clean.

To decorate blend the butter and icing sugar together until light and creamy, then add half the raspberries and blend again.

Using a piping bag pipe the butter cream into the centre of the cake and decorate with the remaining whole raspberries.

Cream Puff with Strawberries

MAKES
12

PREP TIME
35
minutes

COOKING TIME
20-30
minutes

INGREDIENTS

For the cupcakes

85 g / 3 oz / ⅓ cup butter
220 ml / 7 ½ fl. oz / 1 cup water
105 g / 3 ¾ oz / ⅔ cup plain (all-purpose)
flour, well sifted
a pinch of salt
3 eggs, beaten

To decorate

240 ml / 8 fl. oz / 1 cup double cream
3 tbsp icing sugar
24 large strawberries, hulled and halved

METHOD

Preheat the oven to 200°C (fan 180°C) 400F, gas 6.

Put the butter and water into a heavy saucepan. Heat slowly to melt the butter then turn up the heat and bring to a rolling boil.

Sieve the salt and flour 3 times.

When the mixture begins to boil, tip all the flour and salt into the pan and remove from the heat.

Working quickly, beat the mixture hard with a wooden spoon until the mixture leaves the side of the pan.

Spread the mixture onto a plate and leave to cool.

When the mixture is cooler return to the pan and beat in the eggs until soft, shiny and smooth.

The mixture should be dropping consistency and not runny.

Spoon onto a non-stick baking tray into 12 large balls.

Bake in the oven for 20-30 minutes until brown and firm.

Leave to cool before whipping the cream with a little icing sugar.

Cut off the top of the puff, pipe with cream and decorate with strawberries.

Mochaccino Cupcakes

MAKES 12

PREP TIME 25 minutes

COOKING TIME 15-20 minutes

INGREDIENTS

For the cupcakes

110 g / 4 oz / 1 cup self-raising flour, sifted
28 g / 1 oz / ¼ cup unsweetened cocoa powder, sifted
110 g / 4 oz / ½ cup caster (superfine) sugar
110 g / 4 oz / ½ cup butter, softened
2 large eggs
2 tsp instant espresso powder

To decorate

225 ml / 8 fl. oz / 1 cup double (heavy) cream
2 tbsp icing (confectioners') sugar
1 tbsp unsweetened cocoa powder
12 chocolate decorations

METHOD

Preheat the oven to 190°C (170° fan) / 375F / gas 5 and oil 12 espresso cups.

Combine the flour, cocoa, sugar, butter, eggs and vanilla extract in a bowl and whisk together for 2 minutes or until smooth.

Divide the mixture between the espresso cups, stand them on a baking tray and bake in the oven for 15 – 20 minutes.

Test with a wooden toothpick, if it comes out clean, the cakes are done.

Transfer the cakes to a wire rack and leave to cool completely.

To make the topping, whip the cream with the icing sugar until it forms soft peaks.

Spoon the cream into a piping bag fitted with a large star nozzle and pipe a swirl on top of each cake.

Put the cocoa in a small sieve and dust the top of the cakes, then finish with a chocolate decoration.

Black Forest Cupcakes

MAKES
12

PREP
TIME
30
minutes

COOKING
TIME
20
minutes

INGREDIENTS

For the cupcakes

125 g / 4 ½ oz / ½ cup unsalted butter, softened

50 g / 1 ½ oz / ½ cup dark chocolate, chopped

50 g / 1 ½ oz / ½ cup milk chocolate, chopped

300 g / 10 ½ oz / 1 cup cherry jam (jelly)

2 large eggs, gently beaten

150 g / 5 oz / ¾ cup caster (superfine) sugar

150 g / 5 oz / 1 cup self-raising flour

12 cupcake paper cases

To decorate

24 fresh cherries, pitted and cut in half

200 ml double cream

1 tbsp icing sugar

chocolate shards

METHOD

Preheat oven to 180°C (160° fan) 375F, gas 5.

Line a cupcake tray with paper cases.

On a medium heat melt the butter and then add the chocolate. Stir off the heat until both are smooth and blended.

Add the cherry jam sugar, eggs and salt. Stir together.

Fold in the flour and pour into the paper cases.

Cook for 20-25 minutes until dark, golden and risen.

Remove from the tin and leave to cool on a wire rack.

Lightly whip the double cream with the icing sugar until it reaches piping consistency.

Pipe the cream on top of the cupcakes.

Garnish with 2 cherry halves and some chocolate shards.

Vanilla Cranberry Cupcakes

MAKES
24

PREP TIME
25 minutes

COOKING TIME
18-20 minutes

INGREDIENTS

For the cupcakes

175 g / 6 oz / ¾ cup unsalted butter, softened
175 g / 6 oz / 1 ⅛ cups self-raising flour
1 tsp baking powder
3 medium eggs lightly beaten
175 g / 6 oz / ¾ cup golden caster (superfine) sugar
75 g / 2 ½ oz / ½ cup dried cranberries, chopped
1 tsp vanilla extract
24 paper cases

To decorate

400 g / 7 oz / 1 cup unsalted butter
800 g / 14 oz / 3 cups icing sugar, sifted
a little pink food colouring
75 g / 2 ½ oz / ½ cup dried cranberries, chopped

METHOD

Preheat oven to 180°C (160° fan) 375F, gas 5.

Line the cupcake tin with paper cases.

Cream the butter and sugar together in a food processor until pale and fluffy. Add the eggs a little at a time and if the mixture starts to curdle add a little of the flour.

Add the vanilla extract to the mixture together with the dried cranberries.

Spoon the mixture into the cases and bake for 18-20 minutes until risen and golden.

Leave to cool on a wire rack.

To decorate, beat the butter until soft. Add the icing sugar and beat again.

Add a little pink food colouring and spoon onto the cooled cupcakes.

Decorate with the chopped, dried cranberries.

Pomegranate Soft Cakes

MAKES 12

PREP TIME 20 minutes

COOKING TIME 20 minutes

INGREDIENTS

For the cupcakes

120 g / 4 oz / ½ cup unsalted butter, softened
175 g / 6 oz / ⅔ cup caster (superfine) sugar
1 medium egg, lightly beaten
250 g / 9 oz / 1 ¾ cups plain (all-purpose) flour
2 ½ tsp baking powder
½ tsp bicarbonate of (baking) soda
a pinch of salt
300 ml / 11 fl. oz / 1 ⅓ cups plain yoghurt
seeds of 1 large pomegranate
12 paper cases

To decorate

seeds of 1 large pomegranate
seedless raspberry jam

METHOD

Preheat oven to 180°C (160° fan) 375F, gas 5.

Line a 12 hole cupcake tin with paper cases.

Beat the butter and sugar together in a mixing bowl until light and fluffy.

Gradually add in the egg.

Sift in the flour, baking powder, bicarbonate and salt, then stir until just combined.

Carefully stir in the yoghurt and the pomegranate seeds.

Spoon the mixture into the cases and bake for 20 minutes until golden and springy to the touch.

Leave to cool on a wire rack, peel away from the cases then cut each cupcake in half.

To decorate, gently warm the seedless raspberry jam and if necessary let down with a little water.

Spread a little of the warm jam on the top of each cake.

Stir the pomegranate seeds through the remaining jam and sandwich the cakes together with the mixture. Spoon a few seeds on top as a garnish.

Coffee and Chocolate Charlottines

MAKES
10

PREP TIME
30 minutes

COOKING TIME
25 minutes

INGREDIENTS

For the cupcakes

110 g / 4 oz / ½ cup unsalted butter, softened
85 g / 3 oz / ½ cup caster (superfine) sugar
2 tbsp light brown sugar
2 medium eggs
150 g / 5 oz / 1 cup plain (all-purpose) flour
25 g / 1 oz cocoa powder
1 tsp baking powder
a pinch of salt
120 ml / 4 fl. oz / ½ cup whole milk
85 g / 3 oz / ½ cup milk chocolate chips
3 tbsp very strong coffee

To decorate

350 g / 12 oz / 2 cups good quality dark chocolate
3 tbsp vegetable oil
240 ml / 8 fl. oz / 1 cup whipped cream
pink sugar crystals
cocoa powder to dust

METHOD

Preheat oven to 190°C (170° fan) 375F, gas 5.

Grease and line the brownie tray with with greaseproof paper.

Beat the butter and sugars together in a mixing bowl until light and fluffy.

Add the eggs a little at a time beating carefully.

Stir the dry ingredients together and gently stir into the mixture. Stir in the milk, milk chocolate chips and coffee.

Spoon the mixture into the brownie tray and bake for around 25 minutes until risen and firm. Leave to cool before transferring to a wire rack.

Once cooled use a cutter to cut out 10 circular cakes.

To decorate, put the chocolate and oil in a heatproof bowl set over a pan of simmering water and stir until melted. Leave to cool a little.

Holding each cake by the base dip them into the chocolate mixture and leave to set.

Pipe the whipped cream on top of the cakes and sprinkle with sugar crystals and a little cocoa powder.

Pretty

Loveheart Cupcakes

MAKES
12

PREP
TIME
20
minutes

COOKING
TIME
15-20
minutes

INGREDIENTS

For the cupcakes

125 g / 4 ½ oz / ½ cup unsalted butter,
softened
125 g / 4 ½ oz / ⅔ cup soft brown sugar
2 medium eggs
125 g / 4 ½ oz / ¾ cup plain (all-purpose)
flour
½ tsp bicarbonate of (baking) soda
2 tsp baking powder
2 tsp vanilla extract
2-3 tbsp milk
12 paper cupcake cases

To decorate

175 g / 6 oz / 1 ¼ cups icing sugar, sifted
75 g / 2 ½ oz / ⅓ cup butter, softened
½ tsp vanilla extract
heart-shaped sugar sprinkles
tube of red icing with flat nozzle

METHOD

Preheat the oven to 200°C (170° fan) 400F, gas 6.

Put all of the ingredients except the milk in a food processor and blend until smooth.

Add the milk a little at a time and blend again.

Spoon the mixture in the paper cases.

Bake in the oven for 15-20 minutes until dark golden and well risen.

Once cool, gently remove from the paper cases.

Make the topping by creaming together the icing sugar and butter until very pale and fluffy. Add the vanilla extract.

Using a piping bag and star-shaped nozzle, pipe in rounds on top of the cupcake to create a whipped cream effect.

Decorate with heart shaped sprinkles and red icing.

Violet Cupcakes

MAKES
12

PREP TIME
30
minutes

COOKING TIME
15-20
minutes

INGREDIENTS

For the cupcakes

110 g / 4 oz / 1 cup self-raising flour, sifted
110 g / 4 oz / ½ cup caster (superfine) sugar
110 g / 4 oz / ½ cup butter, softened
2 large eggs
1 tbsp violet syrup

To decorate

110 g / 4 oz / ½ cup butter, softened
225 g / 8 oz / 2 cups icing (confectioners')
sugar
2 tbsp violet syrup
edible rice paper flowers and leaves

METHOD

Preheat the oven to 190°C (170° fan) / 375F / gas 5 and line a 12-hole cupcake tin with paper cases.

Combine the flour, sugar, butter, eggs and violet syrup in a bowl and whisk together for 2 minutes or until smooth.

Divide the mixture between the paper cases then transfer the tin to the oven and bake for 15 – 20 minutes.

Test with a wooden toothpick, if it comes out clean, the cakes are done.

Transfer the cakes to a wire rack and leave to cool completely.

To make the buttercream, beat the butter with a wooden spoon until light and fluffy then beat in the icing sugar a quarter at a time.

Use a whisk to incorporate the violet syrup, then whisk for 2 minutes or until smooth and well whipped.

Spoon the icing into a piping bag fitted with a large plain nozzle and pipe a big swirl of icing on top of each cake.

Finish each cake with a rice paper flower and leaf.

Chocolate Cupcakes with Coconut

MAKES
12

PREP TIME
30
minutes

COOKING TIME
20-25
minutes

INGREDIENTS

For the cupcakes

190 g / 6 ¾ oz / 1 ⅓ cups plain (all-purpose) flour

30 g / 1 oz / 2 tbsp cocoa powder

1 ½ tsp baking powder

165 g / 5 ¾ oz / ⅔ cup caster (superfine) sugar

125 g / 4 ½ oz / ½ cup unsalted butter, softened

60 ml / 2 fl. oz / ¼ cup whole milk

3 large eggs

1 tsp vanilla extract

12 cupcake cases

To decorate

240 ml / 8 fl. oz / 1 cup double cream

2 tbsp icing sugar

75 g / 2 ½ oz / ½ cup dessicated coconut

METHOD

Preheat oven to 160°C (140° fan) 325F, gas 3.

Line a cupcake tin with the paper cases.

Sift the flour, cocoa and baking powder into a large bowl.

Add the sugar, butter, milk, eggs and vanilla.

Beat together using an electric whisk until combined and then for a further 2 minutes.

Divide the mixture between the paper cases and bake for 20-25 minutes, until firm to the touch.

Leave to cool in the tin for a few minutes before transferring to a wire rack.

To decorate, gently whip the cream with the icing sugar and half the coconut.

Spoon on to the cupcakes and sprinkle the remaining coconut on top.

Iced Mini Cupcakes

MAKES **36**

PREP TIME **30 minutes**

COOKING TIME **15 minutes**

INGREDIENTS

For the cupcakes
175 g / 6 oz / 1 cup unsalted, butter
175 g / 6 oz / 1 ¼ cup self-raising flour
pinch of salt
2 eggs, lightly beaten
175 g / 6 oz / ¾ cup caster (superfine) sugar
zest and juice of 1 lemon
36 mini paper cases

To decorate
680 g / 14 oz / 4 cups icing sugar, sifted
pink food colouring
orange food colouring
yellow food colouring

METHOD

Preheat oven to 180°C (160° fan) 375F, gas 5.

Line a mini cupcake tin with paper cases.

Sift the flour and salt into a bowl.

Melt the butter in a small pan and leave to cool.

Use an electric beater to mix together the sugar and eggs until light and fluffy.

Blend in the melted butter and then gently fold in the flour and zest and finally the juice.

Pour into the paper cases and bake for 15 minutes.

Leave to cool on a wire rack.

Mix together the icing sugar and a little water. Separate into three batches and colour each batch with a different food colouring.

Pipe onto the cupcakes.

Flower Cupcakes with Rosebuds

MAKES
24

PREP TIME
30
minutes

COOKING TIME
15-20
minutes

INGREDIENTS

For the cupcakes

175 g / 6 oz / ½ cup unsalted butter, softened
175 g / 6 oz / 1 ⅓ cups self-raising flour
1 tsp baking powder
3 medium eggs, lightly beaten
175 g / 6 oz / 1 cup golden caster sugar
1 tsp vanilla extract
24 cupcake cases

To decorate

500 g / 1 lb / 3 cups icing sugar, sifted
6 tbsp lemon juice
½ tsp orange flower water
½ tsp lavender water
½ tsp rosewater
sugar icing flowers

METHOD

Preheat the oven to 180°C (160° fan) 375F, gas 5.

Beat the cupcake ingredients together with an electric whisk.

Line 2 cupcake tins with the cases. Spoon the mixture into the cases but only half fill.

Bake for 15-20 minutes until golden and well risen.

Leave to cool on a wire rack.

Put the icing sugar in a bowl and gradually stir in the lemon juice until the mixture thickly coats the back of a spoon.

Add flower essence to each bowl to taste, using more or less as desired.

Cover each bowl with film to prevent the icing from drying out.

Pour the icing over the cooled cupcakes to create flat surface and leave until nearly set.

Decorate each cupcake with iced sugar flowers.

Valentine Rose Cupcakes

MAKES
12

PREP TIME
30 minutes

COOKING TIME
15-20 minutes

INGREDIENTS

For the cupcakes
110 g / 4 oz / 1 cup self-raising flour, sifted
110 g / 4 oz / ½ cup caster (superfine) sugar
110 g / 4 oz / ½ cup butter, softened
2 large eggs
1 tsp vanilla extract

To decorate
225 g / 8 oz / 2 cups icing (confectioners') sugar
2 – 4 tsp rose water
a few drops of pink food colouring
pink heart-shaped cake sprinkles

METHOD

Preheat the oven to 190°C (170° fan) / 375F / gas 5 and line a 12-hole cupcake tin with paper cases.

Combine the flour, sugar, butter, eggs and vanilla extract in a bowl and whisk together for 2 minutes or until smooth.

Divide the mixture between the paper cases then transfer the tin to the oven and bake for 15 – 20 minutes.

Test with a wooden toothpick, if it comes out clean, the cakes are done.

Transfer the cakes to a wire rack and leave to cool completely.

Sieve the icing sugar into a bowl and stir in just enough rose water to make a thick, spreadable icing.

Spoon the icing onto the cakes, using the back of the spoon to spread it out.

Sprinkle the cakes with heart-shaped cake sprinkles to finish.

Iced Orange Mini Cupcakes

MAKES
20-24

PREP
TIME
30
minutes

COOKING
TIME
20
minutes

INGREDIENTS

For the cupcakes

250 g / 9 oz / 1 cup unsalted butter, softened
250 g / 9 oz / 1 ¼ cups caster (superfine) sugar
250 g / 9 oz / 2 cups self-raising flour, sifted
2 oranges grated and zested
75 ml / 2 ½ fl. oz / ¼ cup orange juice
4 medium eggs lightly beaten

To decorate

200 g / 7 oz / 1 ¾ cup icing sugar, sifted
½ orange, juiced
3 drops orange flower water
24 strips of candied orange peel

METHOD

Preheat the oven to 170°C (150° fan) / 350F / gas 4.

Grease two non-stick cupcake tins.

Cream the butter, sugar and zest until pale, light and fluffy using an electric whisk.

Add the eggs gradually, beating after each addition. If the mixture curdles, add 1 tbsp of the measured flour.

Fold in the remaining flour and slowly mix in the orange juice.

Spoon the mixture into the greased tins.

Bake for 20 minutes until golden and well risen.

Leave to cool for two minutes then turn out from the tin and leave on a wire rack to cool.

To make the icing, put the sifted icing sugar into a bowl and add the orange juice and orange flower water a little at a time, until the mixture coats the back of a spoon.

Using a palette knife, swipe the mixture onto the cooled cakes and decorate with the orange peel.

Raspberry and Rose Cupcakes

MAKES
12

PREP TIME
35
minutes

COOKING TIME
15-20
minutes

INGREDIENTS

For the cupcakes
110 g / 4 oz / 1 cup self-raising flour, sifted
110 g / 4 oz / ½ cup caster (superfine) sugar
110 g / 4 oz / ½ cup butter, softened
2 large eggs
1 tsp rose water
12 fresh raspberries

To decorate
110 g / 4 oz / ½ cup butter, softened
225 g / 8 oz / 2 cups icing (confectioners')
sugar
2 tbsp milk
1 tsp rose water
a few drops of pink food colouring

METHOD

Preheat the oven to 190°C (170° fan) / 375F / gas 5 and line a 12-hole cupcake tin with paper cases.

Combine the flour, sugar, butter, eggs and rose water in a bowl and whisk together for 2 minutes or until smooth.

Divide half of the mixture between the paper cases, then press a raspberry into the centre of each one.

Top with the rest of the cake mixture then transfer the tin to the oven and bake for 15 – 20 minutes.

Test with a wooden toothpick, if it comes out clean, the cakes are done.

Transfer the cakes to a wire rack and leave to cool completely.

To make the buttercream, beat the butter with a wooden spoon until light and fluffy then beat in the icing sugar a quarter at a time.

Use a whisk to incorporate the milk, rose water and food colouring, then whisk for 2 minutes or until smooth and well whipped.

Spoon the icing into a piping bag fitted with a large star nozzle and pipe a big swirl of icing on top of each cake.

Strawberry Swirl Cupcakes

MAKES
12

PREP TIME
35
minutes

COOKING TIME
15-20
minutes

INGREDIENTS

For the cupcakes

110 g / 4 oz / 1 cup self-raising flour, sifted
110 g / 4 oz / ½ cup caster (superfine) sugar
110 g / 4 oz / ½ cup butter, softened
2 large eggs
110 g / 4 oz / ½ cup strawberry jam (jelly)

To decorate

110 g / 4 oz / ½ cup butter, softened
225 g / 8 oz / 2 cups icing (confectioners')
sugar
2 tbsp milk
1 tsp vanilla extract
edible heart sprinkles
a few drops of pink food colouring

METHOD

Preheat the oven to 190°C (170° fan) / 375F / gas 5 and line a 12-hole cupcake tin with paper cases.

Combine the flour, sugar, butter and eggs in a bowl and whisk together for 2 minutes or until smooth.

Divide half of the mixture between the paper cases, then add 1 tsp of strawberry jam in the centre of each one.

Top with the rest of the cake mixture then transfer the tin to the oven and bake for 15 – 20 minutes.

Test with a wooden toothpick, if it comes out clean, the cakes are done.

Transfer the cakes to a wire rack and leave to cool completely.

To make the buttercream, beat the butter with a wooden spoon until light and fluffy then beat in the icing sugar a quarter at a time.

Use a whisk to incorporate the milk, vanilla extract and food colouring, then whisk for 2 minutes or until smooth and well whipped.

Spoon the icing into a piping bag fitted with a large star nozzle and pipe a big swirl of icing on top of each cake. Sprinkle the edible hearts onto the cakes.

White Chocolate Cupcakes

MAKES
12

PREP TIME
30 minutes

COOKING TIME
18-20 minutes

INGREDIENTS

For the cupcakes

100 g / 3 ½ oz / ½ cup unsalted butter, softened
100 g / 3 ½ oz / ½ cup caster (superfine) sugar
100 g / 3 ½ oz / ⅔ cup self-raising flour sifted
2 medium eggs, lightly beaten
1 tsp vanilla essence
1 tsp baking powder

To decorate

2 tbsp whole milk
100 g / 3 ½ oz / 1 cup white chocolate
3 tbsp double cream
200 g / 7 oz / 1 cup cream cheese
40 g / 1 ½ oz / ⅓ cup icing sugar, sifted
star shaped sugar sprinkles

METHOD

Preheat oven to 180°C (160° fan) / 375F / gas 5.

Line a cupcake tin with paper cases.

Cream together the butter and the sugar in a food processor until light and fluffy.

Add the eggs, one at a time and the vanilla extract. Mix again.

Gently fold in the flour and the baking powder.

If the mixture is a little thick add a little milk.

Fill the cupcake cases with the mixture and cook for 15-18 minutes until golden and risen.

Leave to cool on a wire rack.

Make the white chocolate frosting. Melt the chocolate into the cream in a microwave on a gentle heat. Leave to cool for a minute.

Using an electric mixer, beat the cream cheese and sugar together with the melted mixture.

Using a piping bag and nozzle, pipe the mixture onto the cakes and decorate with star shaped sugar sprinkles.

Rose and Vanilla Cupcakes

MAKES
24

PREP TIME
40 minutes

COOKING TIME
20 minutes

INGREDIENTS

For the cupcakes
175 g / 6 oz / ⅔ cup unsalted butter, softened
175 g / 6 oz / 1 ¼ cups self-raising flour
1 tsp baking powder
3 medium eggs lightly beaten
175 g / 6 oz / ⅔ cup golden caster (superfine) sugar
1 tsp vanilla extract
2 drops of pink food colouring

To decorate
175 g / 6 oz / 1 cup icing sugar, sifted
75 g / 2 ½ oz / ⅓ cup butter, softened
½ tsp rosewater
2 drops pink food colour
1 pack of pink fondant icing

METHOD

Preheat the oven to 180°C (160° fan) / 375F / gas 5.

Line a cupcake tin with the paper cases.

Cream together in a food processor the sugar and butter until pale and fluffy. Fold the eggs in one at a time. If the mixture starts to curdle, add a little of the flour.

Add the vanilla extract and 2 drops of food colouring to give the mixture a pale pink colour.

Spoon the mixture into the cases and bake for 18-20 minutes until risen and golden. Leave to cool on a wire rack.

Make the buttercream by blending the sugar and butter until light and airy.

Add 2 drops of food colour together with the rosewater.

Using a piping bag, pipe the buttercream onto the cooled cupcakes.

To make the fondant roses, roll out the icing to a 2 mm thickness. Using a knife cut into strips. Roll a little of each strip together to form small buds.

Using a knife, cut out some small petals out of the fondant icing and thin using your fingers. Attach to the rosebud centre and leave to set.

When the rosebuds have hardened, transfer them to the cakes.

Lemon Cupcakes with Meringue

MAKES
12

PREP TIME
40
minutes

COOKING TIME
18-20
minutes

INGREDIENTS

For the cupcakes

100 g / 3 ½ oz / ½ cup unsalted butter, softened
100 g / 3 ½ oz / ½ cup caster (superfine) sugar
1 tsp vanilla extract
2 medium eggs lightly beaten
100 g / 3 ½ oz / ⅔ cup self-raising flour
1 lemon, zest finely grated
1 tbsp lemon juice
12 cupcake cases

To decorate

2 large egg whites
50 ml / 2 fl. oz water
100 g / 3 ½ oz / ½ cup caster sugar
zest of 1 lemon

METHOD

Preheat the oven to 180°C (160° fan) / 375F / gas 5.

Cream the butter and sugar together until pale and fluffy.

Add the eggs, a little at a time. If the mixture curdles add a little flour.

Add the vanilla extract, lemon zest and lemon juice and then gently fold in the flour.

Fill the paper cases with the mixture and bake in the oven for 18-20 minutes.

Leave to cool on a wire rack.

To make the meringue, dissolve the sugar with the water over a gentle heat, until it reaches boiling point.

Whisk the egg whites with an electric beater until stiff peaks are formed.

Gradually add the sugar syrup whilst continuing to whisk the eggs, being careful that the sugar does not hit the electric beaters.

Once the meringue is glossy and slightly cooled, stir through the lemon zest and pour into the piping bag.

Pipe onto the lemon cakes using a swirling motion.

Place the cakes under a hot grill to achieve a golden colour.

Vanilla Cupcakes

MAKES
24

PREP TIME
20 minutes

COOKING TIME
20 minutes

INGREDIENTS

For the cupcakes
200 g / 7 oz / 1 ½ cups plain (all-purpose) flour, sifted
2 tsp baking powder
200 g / 7 oz / 1 cup golden caster (superfine) sugar
½ tsp salt
100 g / 3 ½ oz / ½ cup unsalted butter, softened
3 medium eggs, lightly beaten
150 ml / 5 fl. oz / ½ cup whole milk
24 cupcake cases

To decorate
120 g / 4 oz / ½ cup unsalted butter, softened
220 g / 8 oz / 1 ¼ cups icing sugar
5 tbsp raspberries
pink food colouring
pink sprinkles

METHOD

Preheat the oven to 180°C (160° fan) / 375F / gas 5. Fill the cupcake trays with the paper cases.

In a bowl add the flour, baking powder, sugar, salt and butter.

Rub together with fingertips until the mixture resembles breadcrumbs.

Whisk together the eggs, milk and vanilla extract and add to the dry ingredients beating together continuously.

Pour the mixture into the paper cases. Bake for 20 minutes until the mixture is firm and risen.

To make the topping beat the butter until soft and add the sifted icing sugar, then beat again.

Pass the raspberries through a sieve and into the mix. Beat again and add a little pink food colouring.

Spoon the mixture onto the cupcakes and sprinkle with pink sprinkles.

Vintage-style Cupcakes

MAKES
12

PREP TIME
30 minutes

COOKING TIME
20 minutes

INGREDIENTS

For the cupcakes

225 g / 8 oz / 1 ¾ cups plain (all-purpose) flour
2 tsp baking powder
½ tsp bicarbonate of (baking) soda
1 medium egg
1 tsp vanilla essence
150 g / 5 oz / ¾ cup caster (superfine) sugar
100 ml / 3 ½ fl. oz / ⅓ cup sunflower oil
250 ml / 8 oz / 2 cups plain yoghurt

To decorate

½ tsp Tylo powder
125 g / 4 oz / ½ cup white fondant icing
1 tbsp icing sugar and water, mixed to a paste

METHOD

Preheat the oven to 180°C (160° fan) / 375F / gas 5.

Fill a cupcake tin with the paper cases.

Sift the dry ingredients into a bowl.

Beat together the wet ingredients in another bowl.

Add the wet ingredients to the dry ingredients.

Pour the batter into the cupcake cases and bake for 18-20 minutes until golden and firm.

Leave to completely cool on a wire rack before decorating.

To decorate, add the Tylo powder to the fondant icing so that it will firm up a little.

Knead thoroughly. Roll out to 3 mm in thickness over the embossing mat.

Cut out with a frilled cookie cutter and use a little icing sugar and water paste to stick to the cupcake.

Confetti Cupcakes

MAKES
12

PREP
TIME
45
minutes

COOKING
TIME
15-20
minutes

INGREDIENTS

For the cupcakes

110 g / 4 oz / 1 cup self-raising flour, sifted
110 g / 4 oz / ½ cup caster (superfine) sugar
110 g / 4 oz / ½ cup butter, softened
2 large eggs
1 tsp vanilla extract

To decorate

110 g / 4 oz / ½ cup butter, softened
225 g / 8 oz / 2 cups icing
(confectioners') sugar
2 tbsp milk
a few drops of pink food colouring
small heart-shaped sweets

METHOD

Preheat the oven to 190°C (170° fan) / 375F / gas 5 and line a 12-hole cupcake tin with paper cases.

Combine the flour, sugar, butter, eggs and vanilla extract in a bowl and whisk together for 2 minutes or until smooth.

Divide the mixture between the paper cases then transfer the tin to the oven and bake for 15 – 20 minutes.

Test with a wooden toothpick, if it comes out clean, the cakes are done.

Transfer the cakes to a wire rack and leave to cool completely.

To make the buttercream, beat the butter with a wooden spoon until light and fluffy then beat in the icing sugar a quarter at a time.

Use a whisk to incorporate the milk and food colouring, then whisk for 2 minutes or until smooth and well whipped.

Spoon the icing into a piping bag fitted with a large star nozzle and pipe a big swirl of icing on top of each cake.

Sprinkle the cakes with the heart-shaped sweets to finish.

Vanilla Cupcakes with Lime

MAKES 24

PREP TIME 25 minutes

COOKING TIME 18-20 minutes

INGREDIENTS

For the cupcakes

175 g / 6 oz / ¾ cup unsalted butter, softened
175 g / 6 oz / 1 ⅛ cups self-raising flour
1 tsp baking powder
3 medium eggs lightly beaten
175 g / 6 oz / ¾ cup golden caster (superfine) sugar
1 tsp vanilla extract
24 paper cases

To decorate

400 g / 7 oz / 1 cup unsalted butter
800 g / 14 oz / 3 cups icing sugar, sifted
5 tbsp lime juice
a few drops green food colouring
yellow sugar crystals
sugar stars

METHOD

Preheat oven to 180°C (160° fan) / 375F / gas 5.

Line cupcake tin with paper cases.

Cream together in a food processor the sugar and butter until pale and fluffy. Add the eggs a little at a time if the mixture starts to curdle add a little of the measured flour.

Add the vanilla extract to the mixture.

Spoon the mixture into the cases and bake for 18-20 minutes until risen and golden.

Leave to cool on a wire rack.

To decorate, beat the butter until soft. Add the icing sugar and beat again.

Slowly add the lime juice and colouring.

Spoon into piping bag and pipe in a circular motion onto the cupcakes.

Sprinkle over the sugar crystals and sugar stars.

Lemon and Chocolate Cupcakes

MAKES 12

PREP TIME 30 minutes

COOKING TIME 18 minutes

INGREDIENTS

For the cupcakes

120 g / 4 ½ oz / ½ cup unsalted butter, softened
150 g / 5 ½ oz / ⅔ cup caster (superfine)sugar
grated zest of 1 lemon
2 large eggs
200 g / 7 oz / 1 ⅓ cups self-raising flour
1 tsp baking powder
125 ml / 4 ½ oz / ½ cup whole milk
50 g / 1 ½ oz / ⅓ cup white chocolate chips

To decorate

120 g / 4 ½ oz / ½ cup unsalted butter, softened
200 g / 7 oz / 1 ⅓ cups icing sugar, sifted
50 g / 1 ¾ oz / ⅓ cup white chocolate
pink food colouring
1 tsp rosewater
pink chocolate chips or chocolate shavings
100 g / 3 ½ oz / ½ cup yellow fondant icing

METHOD

Preheat oven to 180°C (160° fan) / 375F / gas 5. Fill a cupcake tray with the paper cases.

Cream the butter and sugar together in a bowl until light and creamy.

Add the lemon zest and the eggs a little at a time.

Mix half the flour, then half the milk into the creamed mixture and repeat.

Stir in the white chocolate chips.

Spoon the mixture into the cases and bake for around 18 minutes until golden and well risen.

Leave to cool on a wire rack.

Make the butter cream by blending the sugar and butter together until light.

Melt the chocolate in a bowl over a pan of simmering water, leave to cool slightly before adding the rosewater and food colouring.

Fold the chocolate into the buttercream and pipe the mixture onto the cakes.

Roll out the fondant icing to a 3 mm thickness and cut out the stars. To make a double star effect, gently push with a smaller cutter into the bigger star to score a line.

Garnish with pink chocolate chips, or chocolate shavings.

Starry Vanilla Cupcakes

MAKES
24

PREP TIME
20
minutes

COOKING TIME
20
minutes

INGREDIENTS

For the cupcakes

200 g / 7 oz / 1 ½ cups plain (all-purpose) flour, sifted
2 tsp baking powder
200 g / 7 oz / 1 cup golden caster (superfine) sugar
½ tsp salt
100 g / 3 ½ oz / ½ cup unsalted butter, softened
3 medium eggs, lightly beaten
150 ml / 5 fl. oz / ½ cup whole milk
2 tsp vanilla extract
24 cupcake cases

To decorate

120 g / 4 oz ½ cup unsalted butter, softened
220 g / 8 oz / 1 ¼ cups icing sugar
2 tsp vanilla extract
blue fondant icing
glitter sprinkles in assorted colours

METHOD

Preheat oven to 180°C (160° fan) / 375F / gas 5. Fill 2 cupcake trays with the paper cases.

Put the flour, baking powder, sugar, salt and butter in a bowl.

Rub together with your fingertips until the mixture resembles breadcrumbs.

Whisk together the eggs, milk and vanilla extract and add to the dry ingredients, beating together continuously.

Pour the mixture into the pre-prepared cases in the tin.

Bake for around 20 minutes until the mixture is firm and risen.

To make the topping beat the butter until soft and add the sifted icing sugar.

Roll out a little of the blue fondant icing to around 2 mm thickness. Cut out little stars using a cutter or freehand.

Leave to harden for 1-2 hours.

Sprinkle the cakes with edible glitter and top with the blue sugar stars.

Banana Party Cupcakes

MAKES
12

PREP TIME
35 minutes

COOKING TIME
15-20 minutes

INGREDIENTS

For the cupcakes

1 very ripe banana
110 g / 4 oz / 1 cup self-raising flour, sifted
110 g / 4 oz / ½ cup caster (superfine) sugar
110 g / 4 oz / ½ cup butter, softened
2 large eggs

To decorate

1 very ripe banana
110 g / 4 oz / ½ cup butter, softened
225 g / 8 oz / 2 cups icing
(confectioners') sugar
a few drops of pink food colouring
pink heart-shaped cake sprinkles
hundreds and thousands

METHOD

Preheat the oven to 190°C (170° fan) / 375F / gas 5 and line a 12-hole cupcake tin with paper cases.

Blend the banana to a smooth puree in a food processor.

Combine the flour, sugar, butter, eggs and banana puree in a bowl and whisk together for 2 minutes or until smooth.

Divide the mixture between the paper cases.

Transfer the tin to the oven and bake for 15 – 20 minutes.

Test with a wooden toothpick, if it comes out clean, the cakes are done.

Transfer the cakes to a wire rack and leave to cool completely.

Mash the banana then beat into the butter with a wooden spoon until light and fluffy.

Beat in the icing sugar a quarter at a time, then whisk for 2 minutes or until smooth and well whipped.

Add a few drops of pink food colouring to the bowl and marble the colour through with a couple of stirs of the whisk.

Spoon the buttercream into a piping bag fitted with a large star nozzle and pipe a swirl on top of each cake.

Scatter over the cake sprinkles and hundreds and thousands.

Chocolate Raspberry Cupcakes

MAKES 10

PREP TIME 30 minutes

COOKING TIME 25 minutes

INGREDIENTS

For the cupcakes

110 g / 4 oz / ½ cup unsalted butter, softened
85 g / 3 oz / ½ cup caster (superfine) sugar
2 tbsp light brown sugar
2 medium eggs
150 g / 5 oz / 1 cup plain (all-purpose) flour
25 g / 1 oz cocoa powder
1 tsp baking powder
a pinch of salt
120 ml / 4 fl. oz / ½ cup whole milk
85 g / 3 oz / ½ cup milk chocolate, chopped
10 paper cases

To decorate

200 ml / 7 fl. oz double cream lightly whipped
110 g / 3 oz / ½ cup fresh raspberries
3 tbsp raspberry flavour dessert sauce
heart sugar shapes

METHOD

Preheat oven to 190°C (170° fan) / 375F / gas 5.

Line a cupcake tin with paper cases.

Beat the butter and sugars together in a mixing bowl until light and fluffy.

Add the eggs a little at a time, beating carefully.

Stir the dry ingredients together and gently stir into the creamed butter and sugar mixture.

Stir in the milk and chopped milk chocolate.

Spoon the mixture into the paper cases and bake for around 25 minutes until risen and firm.

Leave to cool before transferring to a wire rack.

To decorate push the raspberries through a sieve into the lightly whipped cream and stir through the dessert sauce.

Spoon onto the cooled cupcakes and decorate with the sugar heart shapes.

Chocolate Strawberry Cupcakes

MAKES
12

PREP TIME
35
minutes

COOKING TIME
15-20
minutes

INGREDIENTS

For the cupcakes

110 g / 4 oz / 1 cup self-raising flour, sifted
28 g / 1 oz / ¼ cup unsweetened cocoa powder, sifted
110 g / 4 oz / ½ cup caster (superfine) sugar
110 g / 4 oz / ½ cup butter, softened
2 large eggs
2 tbsp strawberry syrup

To decorate

110 g / 4 oz / ½ cup butter, softened
225 g / 8 oz / 2 cups icing (confectioners') sugar
2 tbsp strawberry syrup
cocoa powder to dust

METHOD

Preheat the oven to 190°C (170° fan) / 375F / gas 5 and line a 12-hole cupcake tin with paper cases.

Combine the flour, cocoa, sugar, butter, eggs and strawberry syrup in a bowl and whisk together for 2 minutes or until smooth.

Divide the mixture between the paper cases, then transfer the tin to the oven and bake for 15 – 20 minutes.

Test with a wooden toothpick, if it comes out clean, the cakes are done.

Transfer the cakes to a wire rack and leave to cool completely.

To make the buttercream, beat the butter with a wooden spoon until light and fluffy then beat in the icing sugar a quarter at a time.

Use a whisk to incorporate the strawberry syrup, then whisk for 2 minutes or until smooth and well whipped.

Spoon the buttercream into a piping bag fitted with a large star nozzle and pipe a swirl on top of each cake then sprinkle with a little cocoa powder to finish.

Raspberry and Lemon Muffins

MAKES
12

PREP TIME
20 minutes

COOKING TIME
18-20 minutes

INGREDIENTS

For the cupcakes
100 g / 3 ½ oz / ½ cup unsalted butter, softened
100 g / 3 ½ oz / ½ cup caster (superfine) sugar
1 tsp vanilla extract
2 medium eggs lightly beaten
100 g / 3 ½ oz / ⅔ cup self-raising flour
1 lemon, zested
1 tbsp lemon juice
150 g / 5 oz / 1 cup fresh raspberries
12 muffin cases

To decorate
120 g / 4 oz / ½ cup unsalted butter, softened
220 g / 8 oz / 1 ¼ cups icing sugar
5 tbsp fresh raspberries
pink food colouring
5 tbsp flaked (slivered) almonds

METHOD

Preheat oven to 180°C (160° fan) / 375F / gas 5.

Cream the butter and sugar together until pale and fluffy.

Add the eggs, a little at a time. If the mixture curdles, add a little flour.

Add the vanilla essence, lemon zest and juice.

Gently fold in the flour and the fresh raspberries.

Fill the paper cases with the mixture and cook in the oven for 18-20 minutes.

Leave to cool on a wire rack.

To make the buttercream mix the butter with the icing sugar until light and fluffy.

Add a little of the pink food colouring. Spoon onto the cooled cupcakes.

Decorate with fresh raspberries and flaked almonds if using.

Blueberry Cupcakes

MAKES
12

PREP TIME
30 minutes

COOKING TIME
20 minutes

INGREDIENTS

For the cupcakes
225 g / 8 oz / 1 ½ cups plain (all-purpose) flour
2tsp baking powder
110 g / 4 oz / ½ cup caster (superfine) sugar
2 medium eggs
1 tsp vanilla extract
100 ml / 3 ½ fl. oz / ½ cup sunflower oil
225 ml / 8 fl. oz / 1 cup whole milk
110 g / 4 oz blueberries
12 paper cases

To decorate
200 g / 7 oz / ¾ cup unsalted butter, softened
400 g / 14 oz / 8 cups icing sugar, sifted
a few drops of blue food colouring
36 fresh blueberries

METHOD

Preheat oven to 180°C (160° fan) / 375F / gas 5.

Place 12 paper cases into a 12 hole cupcake tin.

Sift the baking powder and flour into a mixing bowl and stir in the sugar.

Whisk together the eggs, vanilla and oil in a different bowl until slightly frothy.

Slowly add the milk.

Stir the wet ingredient into the dry then stir in the blueberries gently.

Spoon the mixture into cases and bake in the oven for 20 minutes until golden and well risen.

To decorate, beat the butter until soft then add the icing sugar.

Once blended, stir in a few drops of food colouring.

Swipe onto cupcake and use 3 blueberries per cake as a garnish.

Lemon Cupcakes

MAKES
12

PREP TIME
20 minutes

COOKING TIME
18-20 minutes

INGREDIENTS

For the cupcakes

100 g / 3 ½ oz / ½ cup unsalted butter, softened
100 g / 3 ½ oz / ½ cup caster (superfine) sugar
1 tsp vanilla extract
2 medium eggs lightly beaten
100 g / 3 ½ oz / ⅔ cup self-raising flour
1 lemon, zested
1 tbsp lemon juice

To decorate

200 g / 7 oz / 2 cups icing sugar, sifted
1 lemon, juiced
2 lemons, zested
poppy seeds for garnish

METHOD

Preheat oven to 180°C (160° fan) / 375F / gas 5.

Cream the butter and sugar together until pale and fluffy.

Add the eggs, a little at a time. If the mixture curdles, add a little flour.

Add the vanilla essence lemon zest and juice.

Gently fold in the flour.

Fill the paper cases with the mixture and cook in the oven for 18-20 minutes.

Leave to cool on a wire rack.

Make the icing by combining the icing sugar, lemon juice and a little water, until it reaches piping consistency.

Pipe in circles onto the cake and scatter with poppy seeds and extra lemon zest.

Novelty

Christmas Cupcakes

MAKES
24

PREP
TIME
1 hour 15
minutes

COOKING
TIME
15-20
minutes

INGREDIENTS

For the cupcakes

175 g / 6 oz / ⅔ cup unsalted butter, softened

175 g / 6 oz / 1 ¼ cups self-raising flour

1 tsp baking powder

3 medium eggs lightly beaten

175 g / 6 oz / ¾ cups golden caster (superfine) sugar

1 tsp vanilla extract

To decorate

1 pack of red fondant icing

1 pack of brown fondant icing

1 pack of white fondant icing

1 pack of black fondant icing

1 pack of green fondant icing

1 tube of white royal icing

METHOD

Preheat the oven to 180°C (160° fan) / 375F / gas 5.

Sift the flour and baking powder into a bowl. Slice the butter into chunks and add to the bowl. Add the eggs, sugar and vanilla extract. With an electric whisk beat the ingredients together until blended.

Line 2 cupcake tins with the paper cases and spoon the mixture into the cases. Bake for 15-20 minutes until cooked and well risen. Leave to cool on wire rack.

Mix the icing sugar with a little water until it is a medium consistency. Pour onto cupcakes to form a flat iced surface and then leave to set.

To decorate, mould the fondant icing into festive shapes and creatures as preferred. Leave to set for 1-2 hours.

Alternatively, roll the icing and cut out shapes using festive cutters. Leave to set 1-2 hours.

Pipe with additional icing for detailed effect, such as eyes and beards.

Attach the festive faces to the top of the cupcakes with a little more icing.

Lemon Meringue Cupcake Nests

MAKES
12

PREP TIME
40 minutes

COOKING TIME
15-20 minutes

INGREDIENTS

For the sponge

100 g / 3 ½ oz / ½ cup unsalted butter, softened
100 g / 3 ½ oz / ¾ cup caster (superfine) sugar
1 tsp vanilla extract
2 medium eggs, lightly beaten
100 g / 3 ½ oz / ⅔ cup self-raising flour
zest of 1 lemon
12 cupcake cases

To decorate

1 jar of lemon curd
2 large egg whites
50 ml / 2 fl. oz water
100 g / 3 ½ oz / ½ cup caster sugar
sugar flowers
candied lemon zest

METHOD

Preheat the oven to 180°C (160° fan) / 375F / gas 5.

Line the cupcake tin with paper cases.

Cream together the butter and sugar until pale and fluffy.

Add the vanilla extract and lemon zest and then beat again.

Add the eggs a little at a time. If the mixture starts to curdle, add a tbsp of the flour.

Add the remaining flour and beat again.

Pour the mixture into the cases and bake for 18-20 minutes until golden and firm.

Leave to cool on a wire rack.

Meanwhile, make the meringue topping. Dissolve the sugar in the water over a gentle heat. Once dissolved, cook until the syrup reached boiling point.

Whisk the egg whites until soft peaks are formed.

Add the sugar syrup as you continue to whisk, keep the syrup away from the electric beaters.

Continue whisking until shiny and glossy and the mixture begins to cool.

Pour the mixture into the piping bag.

Spoon a little of the lemon curd onto the cupcake. Pipe the meringue mixture like a beehive on top.

Place the cupcake under a hot grill to achieve a golden effect.

Decorate with candied lemon zest and sugar flowers as desired.

Rock and Roll Chocolate Cupcakes

MAKES
12

PREP TIME
60 minutes

COOKING TIME
20-25 minutes

INGREDIENTS

For the cupcakes

100 g / 3 ½ oz / ½ cup dark chocolate, chopped
175 g / 6 oz / ⅔ cup unsalted butter, softened
225 g / 8 oz / 1 cup caster sugar
3 medium eggs
100 g / 3 ½ oz / ⅔ cup self-raising flour
3 tbsp cocoa powder
pinch of salt
12 paper cupcake cases

To decorate

110 g / 4 oz / ½ cup butter, softened
225 g / 8 oz / 2 cups icing (confectioner's) sugar
1 tsp vanilla extract
1 pack of black fondant icing
2 tbsp icing sugar
patterned chocolate shards

METHOD

Preheat oven to 180°C (160° fan) / 375F / gas 5.

Line a cupcake tin with 12 paper cases.

Put the chocolate and butter in a heatproof bowl and set over water that is simmering not boiling. Stir until the chocolate melts and you have a shiny mixture.

Remove from the heat and stir in the sugar, leave for a few minutes to cool.

With and electric hand mixer beat for 3 minutes.

Add the eggs one at a time, beating after each addition.

Sift the flour, cocoa and salt into a bowl and mix together until blended.

Divide the mixture into the cases and bake for around minutes until well-risen and springy to the touch.

Leave to cool completely before decorating.

Beat the butter and then add the sugar and mix until the mixture is very pale and fluffy, almost white. Add the vanilla extract.

Pipe using a star shaped nozzle onto the cupcakes.

Make a guitar by drawing the instrument freehand onto greaseproof paper. Cut it out.

Roll out a little black icing to 2 mm thickness and cut into the shape using the cut out guitar image. Repeat as desired.

Using a little icing sugar mixed with water pipe the front of the guitar onto the setting black icing. Leave to dry for 1-2 hours.

Crumble some black icing for added effect onto the cupcake.

Once set add the guitar to the cupcake and decorate with chocolate shards.

Spooky Pumpkin Cupcakes

MAKES
12

PREP TIME
60
minutes

COOKING TIME
20
minutes

INGREDIENTS

For the cupcakes

195 g / 6 ½ oz / 1 ¼ cups plain (all-purpose) flour
1 tsp baking powder
½ tsp bicarbonate of (baking) soda
¼ tsp ground cinnamon
¼ tsp mixed spice
pinch of salt
115 g / 4 oz / ⅔ unsalted butter, softened
200 g / 7 oz / 1 ¼ cups granulated sugar
2 large eggs
1 tsp vanilla extract
180 ml / 6 fl. oz / 1 cup canned pumpkin puree

To decorate

225 g / 8 oz / 1 cup icing sugar, sifted
black food colour
orange food colour
handful of flaked (slivered) almonds

For buttercream

150 g / 6 oz unsalted butter, softened
350 g / 12 oz icing (confectioner's) sugar
2 tbsp whole milk
orange food colour
2 tbsp cocoa powder

METHOD

Preheat oven to 170°C (160° fan) / 350F / gas 4.

In a bowl sift the flour and raising agents, spices and salt.

With an electric mixer beat together the butter and sugar until pale and fluffy.

Gradually add the vanilla extract and eggs beating after each addition.

Add some of the flour mixture then beat together.

Add a third of the pumpkin puree.

Alternate additions of the flour and puree three times until all is incorporated.

Fill paper cases and bake for 20 minutes. Cool on a wire rack.

Make the buttercream by blending the butter and sugar until white and fluffy.

Split into three bowls, add orange food colour to one bowl. Leave one white. In the third bowl add the cocoa powder for a brown effect.

Spread the coloured buttercream onto the cupcakes.

Take the paper and draw spooky figures eg: skeleton, cat and spiders web.

Mix the icing sugar with a little water until thick enough to pipe. Split the icing into two batches.

Colour the remaining half of the icing with black food colour. Use the black icing to pipe cat, spider and fly shapes.

Add the almond slivers as the wings of the fly before it sets. Leave to harden. Pipe the finer detail onto the figures. Decorate the cakes with the spooky figures.

Cupcakes with Sugar Figurines

MAKES
12

PREP TIME
25 minutes

COOKING TIME
15-20 minutes

INGREDIENTS

For the cupcakes

175 g / 6 oz / ⅔ cup caster superfine) sugar
175 g / 6 oz / ⅔ cup of butter
3-4 tbsp whole milk
2 medium eggs, beaten
175 g / 6 oz / 1 ⅛ cup plain (all-purpose) flour
1 tsp baking powder
150 g / 5 oz / 1 cup raspberries
12 cupcake cases

To decorate

225 g / 8 oz / 2 cups icing sugar
a few drops of vanilla extract
2-3 tsp hot water
yellow food colouring
blue food colouring
orange food colouring
purple food colouring
sugar paste figures

METHOD

Preheat oven to 180°C (160° fan) / 375F / gas 5. Fill the cupcake tray with the paper cases.

Beat the butter and sugar in a mixing bowl until light and creamy.

Add the milk and eggs a little at a time.

Sift in the flour and baking powder then gently fold into the butter and sugar mixture.

Spoon the mixture into the paper cases but only half fill each one.

Place 2-3 raspberries into each case, then fill with the remaining mixture.

Bake for around 15-20 minutes until golden and firm to the touch.

Leave to cool on a wire rack.

To decorate sift the icing sugar into a bowl and stir in the vanilla extract and a little hot water to create a smooth icing.

Separate the icing into various bowls and add the food colouring to each as desired.

Pour the icing onto the cupcakes leave to set for 10 minutes before sticking the sugar paste figures on top.

Ice Cream Cupcakes

MAKES
20-25

PREP TIME
30 minutes

COOKING TIME
15-17 minutes

INGREDIENTS

For the cupcakes
250 g / 9 oz / 1 ¼ cups unsalted butter, softened
250 g / 9 oz / 1 ¼ cups golden caster (super-fine) sugar
grated zest of 2 large oranges
75 ml / 2 ½ fl. oz / ⅓ cup orange juice
4 eggs, lightly beaten
250 g / 9 oz / 1 ¾ cups self-raising flour, sifted
20-25 ice cream wafer cones

To decorate
300 g / 10 oz / 2 cups, unsalted butter, softened
400 g / 14 oz / 3 cups icing sugar, sifted
2 drops vanilla extract
sugar sprinkles to decorate

METHOD

Preheat the oven to 170°C (150° fan) / 340F / gas 3.

Cream the butter, sugar and zest until very pale, light and fluffy.

Add the eggs a little at a time, beating after each addition.

Add a little flour if necessary to prevent curdling.

Fold in the remaining flour and the orange juice.

Place ice cream cones carefully through slats in the wire rack of your oven, on the middle shelf.

Pour the filling into each cone carefully and cook for 15-17 minutes until springy to the touch.

Leave to cool.

Beat the butter until pale and gradually add the icing sugar and beat until pale and fluffy. Add the vanilla extract.

Using a piping bag pipe the butter cream on top and sprinkle with hundreds and thousands or sugar sprinkles.

Carrot Cupcakes

INGREDIENTS

For the cupcakes

175 g / 6 oz / 1 cup soft brown sugar
2 large eggs
150 ml / 5 fl. oz / ¾ cup sunflower oil
175 g / 6 oz / 1 ¼ cups wholemeal flour
3 tsp baking powder
2 tsp ground cinnamon
1 orange , zest finely grated
200 g / 7 oz carrots, washed and coarsely grated
175 g / 6 oz / ¾ cup sultanas

To decorate

225 g / 8 oz / 1 cup cream cheese
110 g / 4 oz / ½ cup butter, softened
225 g / 8 oz / 2 cups icing (confectioners') sugar
1 tsp vanilla extract
150 g / 5 oz marzipan
orange and green food colouring

METHOD

Preheat the oven to 190°C (170° fan) / 375F / gas 5 and line a 12-hole cupcake tin with paper cases.

Whisk the sugar, eggs and oil together for 3 minutes until thick.

Fold in the flour, baking powder and cinnamon, followed by the orange zest, carrots and sultanas.

Divide the mixture between the paper cases, then transfer the tin to the oven and bake for 20 - 25 minutes.

Test with a wooden toothpick, if it comes out clean, the cakes are done.

Transfer the cakes to a wire rack and leave to cool completely.

To make the icing, beat the cream cheese and butter together with a wooden spoon until light and fluffy then beat in the icing sugar a quarter at a time.

Add the vanilla extract then use a whisk to whip the mixture for 2 minutes or until smooth and light.

Spoon the icing into a piping bag fitted with a large plain nozzle and pipe a swirl on top of each cake.

To make the carrots, knead ¾ of the marzipan with a little orange food colouring until pliable and evenly coloured.

Roll between your hands to make a cone and add the lines with a blunt knife.

Colour the rest of the marzipan green and use to make the stalk, then assemble 1 carrot on top of each cake.

Marshmallow Snowmen Cupcakes

MAKES
12

PREP TIME
35 minutes

COOKING TIME
20-25 minutes

INGREDIENTS

For the cupcakes

55 g / 2 oz / ¼ cup unsalted butter, softened
185 ml / 6 ½ fl. oz / ¾ cup honey
1 medium egg
85 ml / 3 fl. oz / ⅓ cup whole milk
½ tsp vanilla extract
110 g / 4 oz / ¾ cup plain (all-purpose) flour
3 tbsp cocoa powder
¾ tsp bicarbonate (baking) soda
¼ tsp salt
12 cupcake cases

To decorate

150 g / 5 oz / 1 cup dark chocolate, chopped
3 tsp whole milk
85 g / 3 oz / ⅓ cup unsalted butter, softened
125 g / 4 ½ oz / ¾ cup icing sugar
24 marshmallows
mini coloured marshmallows
mixed sweets
liquorice sticks

METHOD

Preheat oven to 180°C (160° fan) / 375F / gas 5. Fill cupcake tray with the paper cases.

Beat the butter in a mixing bowl until light and add the honey a little at a time.

Beat in the egg, vanilla and milk until smooth. Sift in the flour, cocoa, bicarbonate of soda and salt then stir into the butter mixture until well blended.

Spoon the mixture into the cases and bake for 20-25 minutes until springy to the touch.

Remove from the oven and cool completely.

For the topping put the chocolate, milk and butter in a heatproof bowl set over a pan of simmering water until melted. Stir and remove from the heat. Allow to cool a little.

Sift in the icing sugar and beat until smooth. Allow to cool, then pipe in swirls onto the cake.

Using a cocktail stick, put the two marshmallows together and press sweets, liquorice and other candy to create faces as desired.

Warn people about the hidden cocktail stick before they eat the cakes.

Daisy Cupcakes

MAKES
24

PREP TIME
20 minutes

COOKING TIME
20 minutes

INGREDIENTS

For the cupcakes
200 g / 7 oz / 1 ½ cups plain
(all-purpose) flour, sifted
2 tsp baking powder
200 g / 7 oz / 1 cup golden caster
(superfine) sugar
½ tsp salt
100 g / 3 ½ oz / ½ cup unsalted butter,
softened
3 medium eggs, lightly beaten
150 ml / 5 fl. oz / ½ cup whole milk
2 tsp vanilla extract
24 cupcake cases

To decorate
500 g / 1 lb / 3 cups sifted icing sugar
6 tbsp lemon juice
yellow food colour
pink food colour
green food colour
blue food colour
sugar daisies

METHOD

Preheat oven to 180°C (160° fan) / 375F / gas 5. Fill 2 cupcake trays with
the paper cases.

In a bowl add the flour, baking powder, sugar, salt and butter.

Rub it together with your fingertips until the mixture resembles breadcrumbs.

Whisk together the eggs, milk and vanilla extract and add to the dry
ingredients, beating together continuously.

Pour the mixture into the pre-prepared cases in the tin.

Bake for around 20 minutes until the mixture is firm and risen.

Leave the cupcakes to cool on a wire rack.

Once cool, make the topping by adding a little lemon juice and hot water
to the icing sugar.

Keep adding water until a runny texture is achieved.

Separate into bowls and colour as desired.

Pour onto the cakes and leave to set for a few minutes before adding
the daisies to garnish.

INDEX